MW00890295

Stupid Things My Students Say

(Surviving Education With The Modern Teen)

Dr. Euclid Pythagoras

Dr. Euclid Pythagoras

Copyright © 2017 Dr. Euclid Pythagoras

All rights reserved.

ISBN-13: 978-1548426774
ISBN-10:1548426776

CONTENTS

ACKNOWLEDGMENTS

I need to thank my wife, who put up with me losing all my hair teaching, and gave me the free time needed to write all of this nonsense down. My past teachers who inspired me to be as inspiring as they were to me. I need to thank the people at Vox Tuus LLC for the advice and help through this process. Miss K.M. And lastly I need to thank my friends and family who encouraged me to keep teaching, not because they believed I was changing the world, but because they didn't want these stories to end. My friends are selfish.

I would be remiss if I didn't say that I owe a lot of my satirical creativity to the creators of South Park, Rick and Morty, The Simpsons, the movie *Idiocracy*, and of course Mr. Mel Brooks. They've been able to see the ridiculousness of humanity, and poke fun at it long before I could.

While almost all my students agreed to have their nonsensical stories shared in the public realm, I have nonetheless left names intentionally vague or changed to protect the privacy of the teens, as well as the names of school districts, teachers, state, and any other identifying factors. If you happen to believe a story is about you or your child, it's probably not, but that's sad either way you look at it...

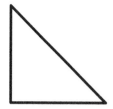

WHY DID I WRITE A BOOK?

This book is the culmination of five years of teaching experience. It is a shameless attempt at supplementing my teaching income. Why? Because teachers make a laughable salary.

You will always hear people say that teachers get all this time off and shouldn't complain. The time off IS awesome, but do you know why we get all that time off? Because if the districts didn't give us that time off, we'd all quit midyear to do literally ANYTHING else! There are some days I must take a sick day so that I don't physically throw a teenager through a window. Spring break isn't for the typical teenager to go play at the beach and enjoy themselves; it's for their safety. A teacher who has literally had their brain broken because little Jimmy has fourteen fidget spinners on his desk, but has yet to bring even ONE pencil to class—that is a dangerous thing.

My wife thinks the paragraph above is a little harsh, and I guess I should preface it by saying that I teach high school, so I'm a little jaded. Elementary school teachers are the sweetest most caring people in the world. They have the most insane optimistic personalities and DO NOT want to beat your children. They were made to do that job. Elementary school teacher in-service is the happiest place on the planet. You would think that they all just came back from Disney World. They truly do love your children, and you know what, I'd argue that most middle school and even half of the high school teachers do too, which is why we take things so personally sometimes.

I have seen phenomenal teachers broken by students—teachers who had the absolute sincerest desires to help students reach their full potential, only to be crushed like a sick and crippled spider under the foot of a ruthless teenager. The teachers cry and ask themselves how kids can be so cruel when all they're trying to do is help them. The veteran teachers might pull out a flask from their desk and offer it to the crumbling newbie who then develops an alcohol dependency just so that they don't go to sleep at night dreaming of the ways in which they would make that student's life hell if they were allowed to take the gloves off.

Many teachers quit. MANY. That word in all caps doesn't even come close to justifying the teacher exodus that happens at the end of every school year, all their hopes and dreams crushed and shattered while tears stream down their face, unsure if the multilevel marketing scheme they've bought into will be enough to get by on. But it seems a better alternative than watching little Johnny spit on the worksheet they've spent hours making at home while having to ignore their spouse, and then watch that post-pubescent nightmare tear it to pieces and throw it all over the floor that you have to clean yourself, even though there is a recycle bin a foot away from him.

If you are a teacher, or were a teacher, you'll read the above and nod your head: "That guy gets it." If you aren't or haven't been, then I probably seem like an enormous asshole. If the latter is the case, I would go through this book and ONLY read the italicized snippets of ridiculous conversations I've had with my students. You might only be mildly upset you wasted money on this book.

This book will not make you a better teacher, and probably not even a better person. In fact, it might make you a worse person who loses all faith in the future of this country. The education system in this country is a joke. It absolutely does not prepare our kids for the future. It is a patchwork system created by a bunch of people who have probably never actually taught, but think they know how it should work, yet end up making it even more convoluted and confusing. "Oh, they added even more content to the scope and sequence of my subject that should take two years to teach well, but they want me to shove it into half a semester, and differentiate it all so that I teach each of my 180 students individually to their preferred method of learning? That seems feasible and intelligently designed…"

I teach high school math by the way; maybe that is where all this bitterness comes from. I teach a class that maybe four percent of the students actually enjoy coming to in the first place before they even meet me. It's not a class you can get deeply philosophical about, at least not without getting a parent phone call or a trip to your appraisers office about why you were trying to convince little Mary that dinosaurs in fact DID exist even though her parents told her they did not.

While I am a bit of a pessimist about the profession, I do love teaching. I love seeing that lightbulb go off in their head when they suddenly realize they aren't terrible at math. I love when past students come back and tell me their success stories, that me pushing them to their literal limit (not pushing them out of their comfort zone, but actually pulverizing it) helped them to become better humans—that feeling is always great. It's the tiny push we teachers need to keep us from completely losing hope. That, and when our principal tells us we get a jeans pass!

I should also say that I consider myself an only-slightly-better-than-mediocre teacher. I have met too many fantastic teachers (my own or those I worked with) who gave me the inspirational push to start teaching and keep teaching. They've found the perfect balance between a personal life and teaching. They have mastered classroom behavior management, and every student would name their firstborn child after them. I have not gotten there, nor do I think I ever could get there professionally. I did win Rookie Teacher of the Year my first year teaching, but I think that was more of a ploy to try to keep me from leaving that economically disadvantaged high school rather than a reflection on my actually teaching.

The following pages are filled with conversations that have taken place over my teaching career. They started as just me venting online, but suddenly developed a cult following on social media. Sometimes the only thing certain people looked forward to when they logged in was finding out "What ridiculous thing did Coach's students say today?"

I sincerely hope you enjoy this book. I hope some of my headaches and hair loss can bring you at least fleeting happiness. If you didn't enjoy this book, teach for a year and then read it again.

THE SARCASTIC TEACHER

One thing you need to know about me is that I am brutally honest with my students. The world isn't going to coddle them. It's not going to tell them they're pretty, and that even though they did poorly in school and have terrible social skills everything is going to be OK. No, I tell them how it is.

Student: Coach, I hate math—this stuff is pointless.

Me: What do you want to be when you grow up?

Student: A doctor.

Me: Ha! You know you're going to need some math and science for that?

Student: No I won't.

Me: Yes you will, and you are terrible at math so you better re-think your life plan.

Student: My mom said I can do anything I put my mind to.

Me: She's lying to you.

Student: What?! You're supposed to tell me I can be anything I dream of.

Me: Oh god no, that is not how life works child. You can't multiply two and twelve without a calculator.

*　*　*

Every single thing I've read about teaching, all the hundreds of hours of professional development, every guest speaker that's been to talk to all of us teachers on those days administrators are just trying to fill time because the "district" says we need to be there...all of those things say that sarcastic teachers are the worst. Kids don't respond well to sarcasm. They need to know they're loved and that you care. They need not be punished. They need gold stars and stickers. Their skin is as thin as tissue paper so we must be careful not to hurt them.

Young kids, sure. I agree. I've been sarcastic with five year olds. It doesn't work. It goes right over their head. Any teacher who's sarcastic with anyone sixth grade and under is just a jackass, but older than that is fair game. The world is sarcastic, so it's just better to get them used to it now. Consider this interaction between me and the world:

World: Hey, here is a nice little tax refund, enjoy!

Me: Oh man that's super cool of you, thanks!

World: Just kidding, you need new tires, your mortgage is due, and you and your wife are having an accidental baby!

Me: You're such an ass.

You can totally be a sarcastic teacher and make it work. The first step is that it needs to be your personality. I've seen teachers try and recreate my teaching style, but they're not the least bit sarcastic in their humor, so they just come off as pretentious or the kids just develop an undying hatred for them. That's not to say I *don't* come off as a pretentious, it's more so that the students understand my extreme sarcasm is how I show that I care for them—by making them feel really stupid sometimes. This is often without much effort on my part.

Student: Coach, are you taking your daughter trick or treating?

Me: Sure am.

Student: You mean "Sure is"

Me: Huh?

Student: You IS taking her trick or treating.

Me: Nope. I AM taking her trick or treating.

Student: I don't think that's right.

Me: Well we're going to just agree to disagree on this one.

* * *

I don't remember my peers being so absent minded when I was in high school. I remember some being quite dumb, but was it the fact that we didn't have cell phones and social media pumped into our lives? It is like an oxygen tank these kids need to survive, and they have no ability to function or problem solve without it. These kids' anxiety is through the roof, and they have so much difficulty figuring things out on their own.

Me: Alright everyone, here is the test review. The key to the review is on my desk to check your work against, and it is also online on the website where you can check it at home if need be.

Student: So can I just go up there and copy it?

Me: No, then you would learn nothing.

Student: But I could when I got home?

Me: Absolutely. It should be a free grade technically, but it won't help you study for the test if you just copy.

Student: I'm going to copy it.

Me: Whatever.

(Next Day)

Me: Alright everyone, turn your reviews in.

Same Student: I don't have mine. Can I turn it in late?

Me: You told me you were just going to straight copy it! How do you not even have it done?

Student: I didn't feel like it.

Me: No, you can't turn it in late. You now have a free zero.

(Fast forward 8 more test reviews later)

Me: Turn your test reviews in.

Same Student: Can I turn it in late?

Me: (takes a deep breath and tries to keep composure)

Student: Coach, can I?

Me: No. In fact you need to go to your parents and apologize, and if they decide to scrap you and start over with a new kid, don't be surprised.

* * *

That's more an example of the sheer laziness that happens in sophomores. They aren't the best at problem solving, but the freshmen are even worse sometimes. Sometimes it's even the players on my own team!

Me: Why are you late?

Player: I didn't know where you all were.

Me: We have practice every morning on the courts unless it is raining!

Player: I thought it was raining so I didn't know where to go.

Me: How did you get to school?

Player: On the bus.

Me: Did you have to get off the bus to get into the locker room?

Player: Yes.

Me: Did you feel water falling on you from the sky?

Player: No.

Me: So was it raining?

Player: I guess not.

Me: Alright, so are you following me yet?

Player: I think.

Me: Spit it back to me, lets see if you got this.

Player: I should have seen the lights on at the courts and realized you were out here.

Me: What?! No. I mean yes that would have been really intelligent, but how did you get anything about the lights from our conversation about the rain?!

Player: Oh, I should have known it wasn't raining because I was outside.

Me: Bingo. We going to keep being late?

Player: Not if we're going to keep having conversations like this.

* * *

One of the most influential teachers in my life was my senior high school English teacher. I think most students will remember their senior high school English teachers. It is the first time that you really don't have to worry too much about standardized tests. You're realistically probably already accepted to college, or have a vague sense of what happens next, and it's a class where speaking openly about your feelings and plans makes complete sense. Not only is that a class where talking about the future is normal, you are probably at least 18 years old, and an adult who should be capable of having adult conversations.

My senior English teacher had his doctorate in something (probably English; I can't remember if he ever told us, or if he was actually a doctor of anything), and the guy had life lessons coming out of his ears. He had seen and done it all. His wall was covered from ceiling to floor with posters of his favorite bands, art he loved, enlarged book covers of his favorite literature, and photos of a younger him riding his motorcycle or protesting for civil rights. The school district actually tried to get him to take it all down and made a new regulation in the district personal guidelines that you had to have wall showing in your classroom. So, he took a small picture frame, took the back off, and hung it between all his mementos so that this small little 4x6 picture frame showed the wall behind it. He wasn't going to let the school board tell him how to influence his students. It was awesome.

I vividly remember him telling us that he had invested his money so intelligently when he was younger, that should he ever be fired from teaching, he'd be totally fine. He taught us how credit cards worked and how taxes worked. He taught us that we know next to nothing and that the only way to expand yourself is to travel and read the words of people who aren't like you. He taught us that feeling uncomfortable is the best way to grow, otherwise you'll only ever stay in your bubble.

It wasn't until I took this class that I really started to come out of my shell as a person. I always played it safe, saying what was necessary to get the job done and nothing more. I worked hard, but I never really took chances. I actually hated to read too. There were books that were banned by the district, but he made us read them anyway. We were teenagers, so of course we wanted to do something that was banned!

One day, I can't remember what I said, but it was dumb enough that this teacher threw an overhead projector at me (not maliciously, he knew I'd catch it), and he made me hold it over my head for most of the class. I didn't think he was being unfair—I figured I deserved it for saying something stupid.

Once, a student brought his backpack into class after being warned multiple times that he wasn't allowed to have backpacks in classrooms. Without hesitation, our teacher walked over to the student, picked up his bag, and threw it out the second story window. The student never brought his bag back to class.

Another time, while in the middle of a lecture, the teacher stopped completely and felt the need to take one of his many plants and throw it out the window as hard as he could into the parking lot where a student was trying to skip class. The student screamed and ran back inside. Who does that?! I don't have a million dollars invested so that being fired would be ok. I also think that the students' parents I have now would sue the pants off me if I hit their kid with a potted plant, but back then it was hilarious and no one dared mess with him.

If this guy could teach us, win awards every year, break the rules from time to time, and have a black belt in sarcasm, I figured I could be at least a little like him.

Student: Coach, do you hunt?

Me: Humans.

Student: What?

Me: I hunt humans, mainly the students who don't pass my class, and are thus worthless.

(Next Day)

Student: I told my parents what you said. My dad says that you're his favorite teacher of mine.

Me: Good. Don't fail.

HOW DID I EVEN BECOME A TEACHER?

I graduated college in 2008 with a degree in Public Relations and a Minor in Sales. I changed my major probably seven times. I had no idea what I wanted to do with my life. I only knew that I was tired of trying to pay for college, and that a degree automatically equaled a job. I was almost right.

I got a job as type of project manager for a small oil company's website job board listing. I should have known I was in for trouble when the vice president of sales said during my interview that my quota was in the millions, but my only product to sell was advertising at about $500 per ad on a website about as attractive as math worksheets are now to my students, but what the hell, I'll take the job. I've got a degree. What can go wrong?

A few months into the first career of my life, oil crashes from $140 a barrel to $40 a barrel, and suddenly myself and my team are all jobless by Christmas. I think to myself, "Not a problem, you have a degree, you'll find another job!"

The optimism finally started to fade after a month of being told repeatedly by hundreds of managers everywhere that they, too, were laying everyone off. I needed a new plan of attack. What does everyone fall back on when they get laid off? Alcohol!

I was always pretty good with money, so instead of developing a drinking habit, I cashed in on everyone else's and became a bartender. That was good for a while. I met some really cool people, most of my friends were still in college and would come visit, but the benefits and salary were lacking. Some of my fellow bartenders and servers decided that they would use their degrees and become teachers. I thought to myself, "Fools! Teachers never make any money!"

After about a year of bartending, the owners of our restaurant decided to shut it down unexpectedly, and once again I was laid off. At this time I still did not teach. I got a job managing a kid's department for a large fitness entity. This was an unwelcome surprise to the entire corporation, so much so that people much higher than my boss were already trying to get rid of me after only a couple weeks. My job title belonged solely to post-kindergarten teachers, daycare managers, and just the generally chirpy happy ultra-optimistic children's T.V. show hosts you're used to seeing work with younger kids. I was not what they were used to. I was all business, management, and profit-loss statements. I didn't need to be Mr. Happy, I needed to be the guy who hired the best Mr. Happy and made a profit at the same time.

I did well my first year, but working for an establishment that is open 24 hours a day, 365 days a year, where the majority of my employees were high school kids or college kids, meant I would go months without a day off, and that was brutally taxing. Around my second year with the company, I was getting burnt out, and with a salary about half of what I make now as a teacher, I knew I needed to get out of there.

When I would work in the child center to help bring down payroll costs, I would find that my dry humor was often very lost on the young elementary school kids, but my teenage employees would find it quite entertaining. It was in the middle of running a summer camp that I decided I would lose my sanity running a camp for elementary level kids and instead should become a teacher of high school kids as it would be less stressful—my logic seemed infallible at the time. That night I called an alternative teaching certification program and the conversation went like this:

Me: I want to be a high school teacher.

Alt. Cert. Program: That's awesome, why?

Me: I want to make more money without having to work every day of the year.

Alt. Cert. Program: OK…what would you like to teach?

Me: Whatever gets me a job the fastest.

Alt. Cert. Program: That would be math or science. What was your degree in?

Me: Neither of those.

Alt. Cert. Program: Well, maybe we can find enough credits in your transcript to make that happen.

Me: Sounds good, work your magic.

Alt. Cert. Program: I think I can find enough math classes, how good are you at Algebra II and Pre-calculus?

Me: Terrible.

Alt. Cert. Program: Well, the demand for young male math teachers right now is extremely high and you'd be almost guaranteed a job if you can pass the math content exam.

Me: Sounds good. Is it hard and when is it?

Alt. Cert. Program: Extremely hard, and in a week.

Me: I have to learn Algebra I through Calculus and AP Statistics in a week?

Alt. Cert. Program: Yes.

Me: Challenge accepted.

I took that exam and passed it with the bare minimum to become a high school math teacher in the state. To this day, the only reason I think I passed that test was out of the extreme need and desperation the state had for new math teachers, and that they assumed I'd figure it out later. To my surprise, hours after I found out I had passed the test, I had three offers to come and teach high school math.

I ended up accepting a job at a high school that wasn't necessarily known for its parent involvement or student achievement, but more so for its free and reduced meals and its proclivity for ending up on the news.

The job did not disappoint. Within my first month working there, we were on the news for a student riot. I'm not kidding when I say riot. I like to exaggerate, but this was, for all intents and purposes, a full on riot. This school was designed around only one extremely large inner hallway that all 4,000 students and teachers had to move through in order to get from one class to the next. This was a school where many gang members attended, and they weren't all in the same gang.

My classroom just so happened to be on the second floor and we had a balcony that looked down onto everything. One little fight between a couple of men during changing periods had escalated into everyone punching and beating everyone else. It was just a sea of wall-to-wall chaos. I couldn't make out a single thing that was happening. Students would run up to me out of breath and say that teachers were fighting students, students were fighting students, and teachers were fighting teachers. I didn't know what to believe, so I just kept teaching Geometry to the kids I did have and figured I'd watch the news later.

A month or so after that fiasco, we were put on lockdown, kind of. We got an email to lock our doors and just keep teaching, so that's what I did. Little did any of us know, a student had brought a gun to school to shoot his fourth period teacher. Luckily someone had ratted him out and he was caught third period. It was at that point when my now wife started to be really worried that my sarcastic nature would get me killed. I don't think she has stopped worrying about this scenario since.

None of these things could deter me though. I still loved teaching even though it was brutally demanding and emotionally exhausting and 78 miles round trip each day for me to get there. Most of these kids had no parental involvement; some of them had no parents at all. It was all of our jobs at that school to convince the ones we could that if they used all of us teachers as their support, we could get them out of the neighborhood that was trying so hard to trap them there. Unfortunately, as hard as we tried, sometimes it just wasn't enough, as can be seen by some of my first social media posts when I was at that school:

Nov. 2, 2012: Days like today, when you know you just changed the entire path of a student's life with one conversation, are why I put up with what I do. One less kid out of jail!

Nov. 12, 2012: Never mind, he went to jail anyway…

* * *

This school also gave me one of the most legendary experiences you get to have as a teacher, one that I am not sure has happened anywhere ever again. Let me give you some background. There was this kid. I can't remember his name, but for this reenactment we'll call him Marco Polo. Marco had so many absences from school that the court ordered his father to come with him to all his classes for a week. When Marco was in class he was quite the distraction to the other students, and I looked forward to his father being here so that this wouldn't happen. Here is how that played out:

(Me teaching the entire class. Marco is talking to his neighbors and distracting everyone.)

Me: Marco, be quiet please while I am teaching.

(Marco continues to talk while I am trying to teach. I give a stern look toward his father who does nothing.)

Me: Marco, last warning—do not disrupt my class again.

(Marco continues to talk)

Me: Alright Marco, go to the office.

(Marco gets his things and heads to the assistant principals office. For some reason Marco's dad stays in my class. As I start to teach again, Marco's dad starts to talk to his friends.)

Me: Mr. Polo, please be quiet while I am teaching.

(Mr. Polo quiets down, but a few minutes later starts to talk to his son's friends again.)

Me: Mr. Polo, if you plan to stay here, I'm going to need for you to not become a distraction in my classroom.

Mr. Polo: I apologize.

(Believe it or not, he starts to become disruptive again)

Me: Sir, that was your last warning. Head on down to the assistant principal's office.

(Marco's father looks sincerely confused and stunned, hangs his head low, and leaves the classroom. I continue to teach for about five minutes until I receive a call on my classroom phone. It's my assistant principal)

AP: I'm sorry to disturb you, but did you refer a parent to the principal's office for discipline?

Me: Yes sir, he was being a distraction.

AP: You can't discipline parents...

Me: He's a grown man who can't follow simple directions; he needs some discipline.

AP: I'm sending them back.

Me: I'll keep kicking them out.

AP: What do you want me to do then?

Me: Put them in In-School Suspension for the rest of the day.

AP: I'll figure something out.

    I'm not sure what happened to Marco or his father the rest of the day, but for the rest of that week, both of those men were perfect angels in class. That school also gave me so many other memorable experiences.

* * *

Me to tardy student: Why are you late?

Student 1: Sorry, there was a fight downstairs and I couldn't get up here.

Student 2: What happened?

Student 1: There were two pregnant girls fighting each other.

Me: What?!

Student 1: Yeah, they were fighting over who gets to keep the baby daddy.

Me: The same high school boy managed to get not one, but two students pregnant and they were fighting each other for who gets to stay with him?

Student 2: That happens all the time.

Me: No, that is not something that happens all the time…

* * *

My first year teaching I didn't have a big following online of the ridiculous things students said yet. I barely wrote them down, I don't know why—they said a lot of ridiculous things, but I am going to have to go from memory on these next couple of stories.

Me: Remember, your final exam counts for 17 percent of your grade, some of you NEED to pass it with flying colors in order to pass the class.

Student: It doesn't matter, my parents won't see my grades until after Christmas anyway and by then I've already got my presents.

Me: You like Christmas, huh?

Student: Yeah, it's pretty much the only time we all get along.

Me: So I'm going to make you a deal.

Student: OK.

Me: If you don't pass this final, I'm going to call your house on Christmas Eve, and tell your parents you failed my class and that you will have to take Geometry in summer school, which will cost them a few hundred dollars.

Student: That's not a deal, that's a threat!

Me: You say "tomato," I say "tomahto"

***

The majority of those students from my first year have graduated by now and are in college. Some have reached back out to me to tell me thanks, and some to show me that they've accomplished more than anyone in their entire family has ever done. One particular group of students heard I was writing this book and decided to remind me of one of their favorite memories.

Past Students: Do you remember Emily? She was tall and super annoying.

Me: Yes I do, wow, I haven't thought of her until now.

Past Students: Do you remember how she always had an excuse to go to the bathroom at least 20 times per week?

Me: Actually yes, that was obnoxious.

Past Students: Well one day you wouldn't let her go because you knew she was just trying to get out of class so she started faking as asthma attack.

Me: What did I do?

Past Students: You took her lunch, which was in a plastic bag, dumped all her food out on the floor, poked some holes in it, and told her to breathe into it.

Me: That does sound like something I would do.

Past Students: It was hilarious, and of course her "attack" immediately stopped and she didn't have to go to the bathroom anymore.

***

Other students came out of the woodwork recently to remind me of other memories they had in my classroom.

Past Student: Do you remember our class would never shut up?

Me: Yes, your class was full of monsters.

Past Student: One day you got really tired of us talking, so you took one of the desks and flung it across the room and it was so loud that the police actually came to make sure everything was alright?

Me: Yeah, that happened so much that they stopped coming to my classroom.

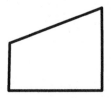

MY SECOND YEAR - THE TRANSITION

I went from one of the most discipline-riddled schools in the city to one of the most prestigious in a year's time. It wasn't that I didn't enjoy those kids, I just couldn't handle that drive anymore. To survive a day in high school education is sometimes a feat of it's own, but then to sit in traffic for another hour to get home…there were days that I almost jumped out of my car and threw someone over one of the enormous overpasses just for not using a blinker.

I also wanted to coach. I had played sports in high school and one of my favorite teachers was also my favorite coach. He was ridiculously sarcastic, but I knew he wasn't doing it to be malicious, it just happened to be how he spoke and how we knew he was being honest with us. He treated us like we were intelligent when we deserved it, and when we weren't, we got called out on it. I wanted to mimic my coaching style after his: he didn't make me want to be better because of him, he made me want to be better because of me. He only solidified the fact that I believed if I wanted greatness, I needed to go out and get it myself, not wait around or do it for anyone else. So when I got an offer to teach and get to coach at the same time, I jumped on it.

At my old school, there were two copiers and all teachers had to make their own copies. What really ended up happening was the machines were always broken. We'd walk in and see the thing jammed and leave before anyone else could see us, otherwise we'd be guilted into trying to fix the damn thing, which we couldn't, and we'd just end up with a ferocious hatred for the copy machine company, and we'd have to change our entire lesson plan because someone tried to put a staple through the damn copier.

This new school had an actual person who was paid a salary to make everyone's copies for them. I was sold on that point alone! I wasn't even allowed to touch a copier. I was so happy, and we worked as a team in our unit to make all the lessons so that no one was solely in charge of doing all the work. It just made sense, but this school was a bit of a culture shock. The student parking was full of cars and trucks worth more than my salary. My old school had a parking lot just as large, but a total of maybe 20 cars. This school had a wait list to even get parking, and even then it was only for seniors.

A few years later I'd be teaching out in the portables. On early release days, all of us teachers would watch the kids drive off in their six-figure vehicles while we struggled with the thought of who we were going to get to jump our cars because we were running on six-year-old batteries. I remember vividly a conversation I had with a student when I first got there.

Student: Coach, what do you drive?

Me: A Nissan.

Student: Like a GT-R?

Me: No way. Those are crazy expensive.

Student: That sucks. I have one.

Me: You're only 14.

Student: I know, but I wanted one so my parents got it for me.

Me: Well that was nice of them, but you can't drive it.

Student: They let me drive it around whenever I feel like it, but I don't really like it that much.

Me inside my head: (punch him, just go over and punch him in the face.)

Me: That's terrible. I feel for you.

Student: Thanks, Coach!

It took some time, but I fell into a rhythm at the new school. The assistant principals were all great, and discipline wasn't exactly an issue like it was in the other schools. Parents did call and email me because they cared how their students were doing. The kids tried because they did actually care about their grades. It felt like I was somewhere that wasn't going to drive me to the five-year breaking point most new teachers get to.

After a few months the principal was hiring a new teacher and they decided I could handle myself. They moved me over to the science wing in an enormous classroom in what felt like the middle of nowhere, so this new teacher could be near the team and learn the ropes since it was mid-year.

It was this separation from the general population where my sarcastic teaching nature started to really flourish because I wasn't afraid of someone popping their head in to check on me. The walls were also concrete instead of a shared wall made of cloth where we could hear everything the other teachers were saying. I was now almost completely free to say and do as I wanted as long as I wasn't committing misdemeanors or felonies.

At this school, not only did I have the normal and expected stupid things that teenagers would say to post on social media, I also had their entirely spoiled nature to vent about. The rest of this chapter includes all the stupid things (and sometimes clever things) that were post-worthy throughout my first year at that school.

Student: My dad just bought me the ps4.

Me: You haven't passed most of your classes all year.

Student: I know, isn't it awesome!

Me: (brain explodes)

* * *

This next little blurb just goes to show you that the students won't always be the ones to give you the trouble. Talk to people who have been teaching for 40 years, and they'll say that it's the parents now. They believe their children are the saviors of this world, and any issues that the school brings to light are purely slanderous and erroneous. I have a million examples of absolute insanity that I have seen parents write to other teachers, lawsuits brought by parents against teachers, and notes written on homework sent back to the teacher preaching about how their child will never have to do that type of work in real life so the parent is excusing their child from having to do it now.

Parent Email: Why did my son get a 60 on his assignment? This is unacceptable. You must have done something or graded wrong. He is a good kid and always succeeds.

My Reply: High school is harder than middle school, but he missed 40% of the questions. 100% minus 40% equals 60%. Have a great day!

* * *

The stories about the crazy things parents say to teachers actually makes me frustrated and angry, so I'll just proceed to give you more of what you actually want—dumb things my students said.

Kid: Coach, I need to be passing!

Me: It's the last day of the six weeks, and you've been failing for five of them. Why are you waiting until now to care?

Kid: I don't know, but what can I do?

Me: Did you study for the re-test I've been telling you about for the last three weeks that replaces ALL your failing test grades with 70's?

Kid: Yes.

Me: Then I wouldn't worry about it. Just take the re-test.

(Student takes test. I grade test.)

Kid: What did I get?

Me: You got a 12. Did you really study?

Kid: No. So what else can I do to pass?

Me: Get away from me…

* * *

Student: Coach, you been around the world?

Me: Not really. I've only been to Israel, took a lot of pictures.

Student: You took pictures of Amish people?

* * *

Student: What is that shape you're drawing?

Me: The square?

Student: No, the other thing!

Me: The circle?

Student: NO! The weird shape! What is that?

Me: This?

The Whole Class: YES! What is that?!

Me: …That's a cursive "d."

* * *

Student: Coach, this isn't wrong, you marked it wrong.

Me: 80 minus 20 isn't 40…

Student: Yes it is.

Me: You know what? You're right. It's all of math that's been wrong for thousands of years obviously. Good catch.

Student: Are you being sarcastic?

* * *

Student: Coach, what's that line called?

Me: That's line Z, as in zebra.

Student: Oh, what's that other line?

Other Student: Line K, as in candy! Geez you idiot.

* * *

Student: Coach, Student #2 doesn't know what a scale is.

Me: Like a fish's scales or a scale you weigh things on?

Student: Like the one I have at home you weigh little things on.

Me: I'm pretty sure you're not portioning out your meals so why do you have a scale like that?

Student: Umm…never mind.

Random Student: Drugs!

Me: Yeah, no, I got that.

* * *

Student 1: Coach, do mushrooms grow on poop?

Me: They grow on decaying matter. I'm sure there are some out there that grow on feces.

Student 2: Wait? So if I poop in my yard stuff will grow on it?

Me: Yes, certain fungi will grow on it.

Student 1: So if I bury my poop, a plant will grow?

Student 2: I'm going to go home and bury my poop and I'll grow a poop tree!

Student 1: I'm going to grow mine bigger than yours!

Me: You know where all those big trees come from in California?

Students 1 & 2: Where?

Me: Dinosaur poop.

Students: OHHHH, that makes sense!

* * *

(The bell has rung to leave class, and a lone student is still sitting in her chair)

Me: Why are you still here?

Student: My shoes are untied.

Me: So tie them…?

Student: I don't know how.

Me: You're 16, what are you talking about!?

Student: They always just come undone!

(I watch and sure enough the kid can't tie her shoes. So I tie them for her.)

Me: What kind of parents never taught you to tie your shoes!?

Student: My mom only wears heels and my dad doesn't wear shoes.

Me: Interesting…

* * *

(Student gets up to write on my board. I let him to see where it goes.)

Student writes: "Math Suck's"

Me: Why did you make "Suck" possessive?

(Student erases the apostrophe, and the S, leaving "Math Suck")

Student: There, better?

Me: Yes, thank you.

* * *

(Student has been playing with a spot on her face all class period)

Student: Coach is this a pimple?

Me: No, that's your face piercing.

Student: Oh, I've been trying to pop it for an hour!

Me: Gross. Get away from me.

* * *

(I turn around from helping a kid with a problem and see a child with a chair over his head)

Me (calmly): What are you doing?

Student 1: He said "Bet you won't hit me with a chair" so I was going to hit him with this chair.

Student 2: I did say that, Coach.

Me (I pause for moment): Alright get it over with then.

Students 1 & 2 (confused): Really?

Me: As long as both of you promise to never have offspring, I'll allow it.

Student 1 & 2: We'll just do our worksheet.

* * *

Me to Student: If I asked you to give me your phone right now or cut off your hand, which would you do?

Student: Phone.

Me: What about if I kept the phone for a week?

Student: Hand.

* * *

Me: Alright everyone, it's time for the quiz. Josh put up your phone!

Josh: Hold on, I'm almost done.

Class: (Hushed suspense)

Me: (Death stare)

Josh: I'll go to the office.

* * *

(This letter was under my door when I got into class.)

"Coach, please pass me. I want to be a physician's assistant or a nurse or something in the FBI, but if you don't bump my semester average to an 80, I'll probably drop out, experiment with sedatives and MDMA, and after a short regretful life—an accidental overdose, I'll leave behind a cat, brother, and ashamed parents. But for only four extra points on my six week's grade, you could prevent a life savings of college money from going to a street pharmacist."

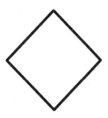

MY THIRD YEAR - THE GOLDEN YEAR FOR STUPIDITY

At this point in my life, I had bought a house with my fiancé so I was really close to the school and not having to spend a half hour driving to and fro everyday. It also meant that I could be a little more involved in my student's extra curricular activities because it didn't mean having to fight through rush hour traffic anymore.

If you want to make a dent in a student's life, go to their games, their matches, their theatre productions, etc. It means the world to them. If you want to see some of the most influential teachers in a school, go to the teacher appreciation nights at these events; you'll always see the same teachers year after year. I get invited to a bunch of these, and I always get some strange looks from the other teachers like, "How the hell is he here again? Does he pay these students?"

This school year I ended up getting the best schedule I ever had. I finally had an off period. I was put in the portables so I actually had a window in my room. You could open it and get fresh air. You have no idea how teaching inside a concrete cube can make you insane—those fluorescent lights all day making your eyes go numb, and all you do is pray for the sound of extremely heavy rain so your brain can reminisce about what it's like to be able to see outside. One awesome thing about this particular portable was the way it faced. I could see from at least 100 feet any superior that was coming my way, so I could get the class to calm down or get them ready for a random appraisal.

This year I also found out that my fiancé and I were expecting a baby.

I knew that this would be the last year teaching where I could expect to get any decent amount of sleep, and it might even be the last year I taught since I would need to make more money to actually afford a family.

Every year you either get smart kids or dumb kids. The year before, my students were pretty dumb. It felt like they didn't know anything math-related and were just giant behavior issues. This year they were actually OK at math. They could generally add and subtract, and none of my classes were better or worse than the others. It made teaching a little easier and less stressful.

While this year was the best for teaching, these kids said some of the dumbest things I had ever heard. It's like they couldn't be good at math AND life, it was one or the other with them. This was the year that my online statuses about the conversations I had with my students really gained some traction, and it started with one of the most ridiculous things I ever heard. This exchange was how I knew it was going to be an interesting year. Some of my friends still bring this event up and use it to introduce me to new colleagues to this very day.

Me: For those of you color-seeing people, please feel free to bring map pencils for the assignment tomorrow.

Student 1: Are you colorblind?

Me: Yes.

(Class freaks out)

Student 2: Whoa, whoa, hold up, hold on, everyone be quiet.

(Class quiets down)

Student 2: Coach, did you know I was black?

* * *

I wish I could say that the student who said the previous is responsible for most of the following posts, but unfortunately that is not the case. Out of about 180 students, the following posts this particular year were spread out evenly between about half of them.

Me to students: It is important in life that, if you're ever in an elevator with a superior, you have a 30-second elevator speech in which you can describe yourself in three words. Would anyone like to try?

Student: Tall, Intelligent—

Me: Let me stop you right there.

* * *

(Student 1 goes and gets calculator and returns to partner.)

Student 1 to Student 2: See if this works.

Student 2: Why didn't you just turn it on while you were over there?

Student 1: What do I look like, some kind of technologist? I'm pretty! I don't need to know how to do stuff.

* * *

Me to Students: Once you're done with the front, raise your hand, I'll check it, and then you can move onto the back.

Student: What's the back?

Me: The opposite of the front…

* * *

Me: Why are your lines so messy? Use the ruler.

Student: I have steady hands, I don't need one.

Me: It looks like a toddler grabbed a pencil and was violently shaken while also trying to write words on your paper.

Student: It doesn't look that bad.

Me: What do you want to do when you get older?

Student: I want to be a surgeon.

Me: Not with those lines…

* * *

Student 1: The answer is 48, you multiply 24 and 2.

Student 2: That doesn't work, you have to add 24 and 24.

Both Students: Which is right, Coach?

Me: Are you asking if 24 x 2 and 24 + 24 get the same answer?

Both Students: Yes.

Me: The system has failed you both.

* * *

(Watching AP video about school policies)

Student: I have a question.

Me: OK.

Student: I know it says you can't bring drugs to school, but what if you do them before you come to school? Is that still against the rules?

* * *

(Watching a video from the AP's about dress code)

Male Student: Coach, why do they care so much about dress code?

Me: Because even a bare shoulder sends your pubescent hormones into a rage.

Female Student: Yeah, we dress like hookers.

* * *

Student: Coach, I have those pants.

Me: Really?

Student: Except they're shorts.

Me: (Blank stare)

* * *

Student 1 to Student 2: Did you see that fight this weekend?

Student 2: No. Was you there?

Me: WERE you there.

Student 1: That doesn't make sense Coach.

Me: Ugh...

* * *

Student to Other Student: Don't judge me based on who I am.

Me: Wait what? That's the only way she should judge you!

* * *

(Student picks up Ninja Turtles action figure off my desk: Leonardo holding swords)

Student: Are you going to give this to your daughter when she is born?

Me: Maybe.

Student (waves turtle around): Pew Pew Pew.

Me: Those are swords. They don't make gun sounds...

* * *

Student: Coach, how do I know if the sides of the triangle are the same length?

Me: What does each side say?

Student: 14in, 16in, 19in.

Me: So...

Student: So...yes?

* * *

Student 1: Coach, why are you eating a sandwich?

Me: Because I am hungry.

Student 2: What's in it?

Me: The tears of children who ask dumb questions.

Student 2: Oh.

* * *

Student: Coach your poster is upside down.

Me: I know.

Student: Can I fix it? I'm STD.

Me: You mean OCD.

Student: What's the difference?

Me: So so much.

* * *

Student: Coach, why is there a smoke detector in your classroom?

Me: In case there is a fire…?

Student: Who would light a fire in a classroom?

Me: You.

* * *

(Two students, a girl and a boy, walk by)

Me (mildly sarcastic): You two look so cute together!

Boy: Gross!

Girl: Gross? Why is that gross?!

Boy: I meant Coach was being gross. You're not—

(Girl storms off)

Boy: I screwed that up, didn't I?

Me: You sure did.

* * *

Sometimes, students who didn't have me for a teacher go on to become adults who work at hardware stores. In the next scenario, I was trying to buy a 2ft x 4ft piece of plywood. Unfortunately it had two barcodes. One said 2ft x 4ft the other barcode said 4ft x 8ft. These people would have benefited from my sarcasm at an earlier age.

Cashier: I have to get a manager to tell me which barcode is correct.

Me: Why?

Cashier: I don't know which one is right.

Me: How tall are you?

Cashier: 5'2"

Me: So not taller than eight feet?

Cashier: I don't get it.

Me: Never mind.

* * *

(I overhear two students while they walk past my classroom.)

Girl to Other Girl: She thought she was being sneaky trying to talk all non-CHANT-ly.

Me interrupting: Are you saying it like that on purpose?

Girl: What?

Me: The word "nonchalantly."

Girl: Are you speaking English right now?

Me: Go away.

* * *

(I overhear one student venting to another student for the millionth time.)

Me: Why does your life always sound like it is filled with drama?

Student: It's not. My life is filled with real.

Me: Real what?

Student: Real.

Me: I don't think you're using your slang right.

* * *

Student: My dad said I could have 10 people over for a party. I invited 50! The house was trashed. He was super angry.

Me: I would be too.

Student: I told him to shut up and go buy me a car. You know what happened?

Me: He punched you in the head? Murdered the original you and built a clone so that he wouldn't go to jail for murder? Built a time machine so he could beat you to death repeatedly, and the "you" standing before me is the only iteration in a multiverse he spared from his rage?

Student: Haha no, he bought me a new Cadillac CTS-V.

* * *

Student: Coach, I just swallowed my pencil. Is that bad?

Me: You'll probably just poop it out.

Student: Oh good.

Me: Or you'll die of internal bleeding trying.

Student: Wait, what!?

* * *

(Student waiting outside my door after school is released)

Me: Where were you today? You missed a test.

Student: At home dyeing my hair.

Me. You missed all of school so you could dye your hair?

Student: Yes. Why? Is that weird?

* * *

Student: Coach, you look like Jesus.

Me: What? Why? I'm wearing slacks and a sweater.

Student: Exactly.

Me: Your only criteria for Jesus is dressing well?

Student: Well you also have a beard.

* * *

Me: Did everyone hand in their graded quizzes?

Class: No, Student 1 still has theirs.

Me: What's taking so long?

Student 1: I don't know how to write an 85 with a highlighter.

Me: It's the same as with any other writing utensil!

* * *

(Bell rings and student is waiting in class looking out the window emotionally.)

Me: You break up with your girlfriend?

Student: Yes. Do you want to know why?

Me: Not really.

Student: Anyway, me and my friend and her were out smoking weed and we got caught by the cops. We lied and said we were baseball players and we'd lose our scholarships so they let us go.

Me: Ugh.

Student: The cops took her home and then her parents called mine and were all angry. I don't need a girl with drama like that in my life. I want a girl who can spend the night and her parents don't care. Mine don't.

Me: How old are you?

Student: 16.

Me: Good luck with that.

* * *

(Sixth Period is taking their final exam. Started at 12:42pm. Final ends at 2:30pm. It is now 2:07pm.)

Student: Coach, I need a pencil.

Entire Class: Are you kidding me?! What is wrong with you!?

Student: I didn't have a pencil.

Entire Class: So you just weren't going to take the final?!

Student: I guess.

(Fast forward two years. I am talking to a former student about what happened to this kid. He ended up accidentally breeding.)

* * *

Student: I need help on my test.

Me: OK.

Student: I can't figure this out.

Me: OK, what is 1 x 180?

Student: 180.

Me: OK, what is 2 x 180?

Student: 160.

Me: How does that make sense!?

* * *

41

Me: Why are you doing your Chemistry review in my class?

Student: Because it's due next class. I know, I know, I should have done it over the weekend.

Me: But?

Student: I was waiting in line all weekend for the new Jordans.

Me: Did you get them?

Student: No, I was waiting in line for a ticket so that I can possibly get them in the future.

Me: (Silence)

Student: You don't have anything sarcastic to say?

Me: I don't know, I mean, I feel like I should have plenty…I think you just broke my brain.

* * *

Me to class: How many places after the decimal is the thousandths place?

Student 1: FOUR!

Student 2: TWO!

Me: It's three…

Student 1 to Student 2: You're an idiot.

Student 2 to Student 1: You were wrong too!

Student 1 to Student 2: But you were more wrong!

Me (shaking head): You were both the same amount wrong!

* * *

Student 1: Coach, I wish there was something to make it warm outside.

Student 2: It's called the SUN you idiot!

Me: Ha!

Student 1: No, I mean like a robot that follows you around and keeps you warm.

Me: Or a warmer jacket perhaps?

Student 1: Are you going to ignore the fact that he called me an idiot?

Me: You're lucky *I* didn't.

* * *

(We're grading papers and going over homework. I see student writing in the answers.)

Me: You know I can see you writing in the answers?

Student: So. How do you know I didn't do it?

Me: Because you're literally still writing in the answers as I'm standing next to you, talking to you, watching you write in the answers.

Student: Dude, come on, this is my third time in Geometry.

Me: Obviously.

* * *

I get this next little blurb said to me at least once a month. It used to make me laugh, but now after so many years, it takes everything in me to keep from shaking them violently.

Student: Coach I have a question?

Me: Ok, what's your question?

Student: I don't understand!

(Silence)

Student: Well?!

Me: That's not even a question!

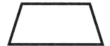

MY THIRD YEAR - SECOND SEMESTER

That first semester was mentally taxing, more so than any semester had been previously. Not only were my students just saying so much dumb stuff that I was forced to constantly think of witty retorts, but my wife's pregnancy anxiety was through the roof. Talking to her drove her mad, not talking to her drove her mad, offering her food drove her mad, not offering food drove her mad, the only thing that actually made her feel better was to sit and watch every episode of FRIENDS on Netflix after I got home from work. I saw every episode 10 times that pregnancy. I wish I was exaggerating, but I'm not. I could quote it in my sleep. I was having an equal amount of dreams and nightmares revolving around red sweaters and nasally ex-girlfriends.

There was one thing that I was allowed to do that didn't drive my wife insane—garden.

(After I read her this last sentence, while in the midst of writing this book, she said that it did in fact drive her crazy, and that she hates the backyard, and that she intends to pave it, but I'm going to leave my previous thought in here because I want to show all the husbands out there: we think we're doing right, but we can't win during pregnancy. We're going to get it all wrong. Don't worry about it. They're growing tiny humans and we're just punching bags who bring them food. We'll literally never know what they're going through, and don't you ever dare say that you do unless you want to be murdered in your sleep.)

I threw myself into gardening. I was growing spinach and jalapeños and satsumas and pomegranates and just a smorgasbord of different edibles until one day they started disappearing. First all the spinach and lettuce started to disappear. I assumed it was wild rabbits. I tried to catch them in the act, but I never saw them. Suddenly, the satsumas started disappearing too. Rabbits don't climb and eat orange trees, so now I was starting to suspect maybe raccoons. Once the satsumas and all the leafy veggies ran out, whatever it was had started to eat all of the jalapeños! I ran into the backyard with a headlamp and a tomahawk and a large camping knife ready to destroy whatever had decimated my garden within a few days time. I waited hours, quietly stalking from the far corner of the yard, but nothing. With all options exhausted that I could think of, I called my local plant store. As you can see, my crazy conversations are not limited to school.

Me: What would eat my lettuce and spinach?

Plant Store: Rabbits.

Me: OK, that's what I thought. What about that AND oranges?

Plant Store: Raccoons.

Me: OK, that's what I thought too, but what about all of that AND jalapeños?!

Plant Store: Parrots.

Me: Is that a thing? Parrot infestations?

Plant Store: That, or your neighbors are just messing with you in the middle of the night.

I decided to go get a live trap and see what in the world was eating (ate) my garden. I stuck peanut butter inside and put it out right before sunset. Within minutes of me going back inside, the dogs were losing their mind at the back door and I looked out to see a cage rattling all over the place. Lo and behold, it was a giant rat. We live in a subdivision, but this is a new subdivision, and all this new construction scared the coyotes, hawks, and owls away, leaving just the undesirables behind.

I drove miles away to some land and let the rat go so it could be food for a hungry predator, then drove home. I set the trap back out and within seconds caught more of these rats. Eventually after leaving the trap out all night and catching nothing, the pests were expelled and I could start gardening once more. I can only imagine my wife's brain when I told her I could not watch TV with her; I had to go give some rats a ride somewhere.

After the rat fiasco and around the time second semester started, sleep was starting to become scarce. I am a light sleeper and my poor wife had a giant baby inside her that loved to do karate on her bladder every few minutes. So while I wasn't the one suffering per se, I was waking up every so often to the sound of flushing toilets. I could write an entirely new book about the ridiculous atrocities committed during marriage and pregnancy, and maybe I will, but for now, I'll stick to what you all came here for.

Sleep deprivation plus dealing with teenagers equals some bad thoughts. This new concoction mixed with an entirely new semester of students who hadn't quite learned what they should and shouldn't say to me resulted in some ideas about getting out of teaching. Quitting finally seemed like an actual option for my mental wellbeing. The little things that would normally make me chuckle inside now made me feel angry and vengeful. Instead of feeling like the kids were just teenagers who do dumb things, they started to feel like incredibly disrespectful children who thought they were adults.

(First day back at school from winter break and I am giving a brief lecture about today's lesson. I see a new student not writing down what she is supposed to; instead she's looking at her phone.)

Me: It's hard to take notes when you're watching North Korean propaganda on your phone.

Student: How did you know I was watching "The Interview?"

Me: I didn't, but now I do.

Student: Can I finish it?

Me: You and I are going to have a fun year.

* * *

Student: Coach, I can't find my calculator.

47

Me: What number is it?

Student: 11

Me: It's right here in front of you.

Student: Oh, it was upside down so I couldn't tell.

Me: IT'S THE SAME NUMBER UPSIDE DOWN!

* * *

Student: Coach, what are you eating?

Me: Shh, finish your test.

Student: I just want to know what you're munching on?

Me: Finish your test and stop talking.

Student: Just tell me what you're eating!

Me: Your hopes and dreams if you don't pass that test.

* * *

Me to Student: Don't talk, there are still quizzes out.

(Student keeps talking to other student.)

Me: Why are you still talking?

Student: I felt like it.

Me: Ha! Did you just try and challenge my authority in my own classroom?

Student: Why are you laughing?

Me: I'm in quite the vengeful mood today.

Student: Please don't call my parents.

Me: I'll do you one better. You're pretty excited to go on your Disney World trip for Band right?

Student: Yes.

Me: I know because it's all you've been talking about.

Student: Don't tell my band director.

Me: I'll do you one even better. I'm going to do everything in my power to chaperone that trip.

Student: Please don't.

Me: I'll never once leave your side. We'll ride every little kid ride I want to ride together, we'll eat everywhere I want to eat, we'll spend all day finding characters to pose in photos with. We'll sit next to each other on the 24-hour bus ride there and back. I'll call your mom every day and tell her what an awesome time we are having. I'll become best friends with your friends and family. I'll be so far embedded into your life they'll start calling me Uncle Mr. Coach. I'll be invited to all your family gatherings from now on. I'll give speeches at special events instead of you. I'll get more and better presents than you at Christmas. I'll replace you...

Student: Please just call my parents now instead, I'm sorry!

* * *

Student: Coach, is perimeter the add-y one or the multiply-y one?

Me (frustrated): What do your notes say?

Student: The add-y one.

Me: Yes, the one you use ADDITION on.

Student: So I add these two?

Me: Yes, you add 4 + 4

Student: 12?

Me: No. What? How did you get 12?

Student: 4 times 4.

Me: That's 16. AND you just said you should add them.

Student: Oh yeah, OK, so 6.

Me (losing my mind): So you think 4 + 4 is 6 and 4 x 4 is 12?

Student: Yes.

Me: You are making my job very difficult today.

* * *

Student: Coach, I can't go to the gym—it's too far, it's like 20 miles.

Me: It's only two miles.

Student: I walk so it's farther.

Me: The distance doesn't magically change whether you're driving or walking or flying, it's still two miles.

Student: Really?

* * *

Player: Coach, why aren't we outside?

Me: It's raining.

Player: Men?

Me: What?

Player: It's raining men outside?

Me: Go do push-ups.

* * *

(Student eating Pop Tarts in my class)

Me: You know you're not supposed to eat in my class.

Student: It's fine, I'm not making that much of a mess.

(I walk over to the student)

Student: What? Bet you won't do anything.

(I take entire Pop Tart and eat the whole thing in two bites)

Me: What did we learn?

Student: Gambling is bad.

Me: Gambling is bad.

* * *

Student: I can't wait to go to prom.

Me: You're going to prom?

Student: Yeah, why?

Me: Out of seven classes, your highest average is a 43%. You've failed my class with a 12% the last two six weeks. You've been suspended four times for fighting. You're 18 years old in freshman classes, your parents are totally cool with sending you to prom?

Student: Yes, I don't see your point.

Me: I'm just kidding, go have a blast!

* * *

I watch and listen to the news daily, read lines of people behind keyboards as they argue and debate one another. There are tons of issues that should be debated, but why is the world so hung up on LGBTQ and all the other letters that come after it? Who cares? My students continue to say dumb stuff constantly, but not a single one cares about anyone's sexual orientation, and of that I am proud.

Student 1: Did you know I was a lesbian?

Me: I never really thought about it.

Student 2: Did you know I was gay?

Me: I think more about y'alls' grades in my class than your sexual orientation, and to be honest, I don't care. You're all weird teenagers anyway. The only time I am ever going to care about who you date is if they're hurting you. Then you come and get me.

* * *

I have plenty of friends who tell me that my classes must be full of idiots. To the contrary, I have some brilliant kiddos mentally. Many will outshine me in mathematical ability probably by the time they are juniors and seniors, but one thing that will always mess your academics up in high school is dating. I continually tell my students that I am miserable at Algebra II because I couldn't get girls off my mind and learned absolutely nothing.

My three smartest students were all females this particular year, and for some reason all of their demeanors started to change. I did some digging and found out they were all dating someone, so I decided to keep track of their grades for research purposes. You can extrapolate from this information what you will:

Top three female student test averages with no boyfriend: 99, 105, 97
Top three female student test averages with boyfriend: 76, 70, 69
Top three female student test averages after relationship ends: 50, 65, 45

MY FOURTH YEAR - THE YEAR WITH NO SLEEP

This was a complex year. My child was about 4 months old. She didn't sleep well, wouldn't take a pacifier or a bottle, and only slept in my arms if I walked counter clockwise around an elliptical piece of carpet in her room. If I attempted to switch directions out of sheer boredom she'd wake up and scream and I'd have to start all over again.

To say there was sleep deprivation is totally correct. My wife has told me about people who have newborns that sleep through the night, and I think they must be lying—that can't possibly be a thing. If you are a parent, you know about the exhaustion. If you aren't one yet, myself and every parent you know will joke and tell you to get sleep now while you can. It's like a curse that one must pass on to the next person otherwise they'll forever never sleep.

While the no sleeping thing was taking its toll on me, I was handed a weird set of classes. Let me explain. There are totally different types of students. Some are labeled special ed, which could mean that they have a math learning disability but are otherwise totally fine, or they might have a level of autism or some other issue. Really it could be any one of an infinite amount of things, but they get mixed into your regular set of kids. Then there is this thing called 504, and dyslexia, and SSL; again, all different types of students that have a whole set of meetings and paperwork that must be completed constantly. ALL of these students have to be taught a certain way. Some might have to have their tests read to them. Some of them might have to have words translated, some need an extra day to complete an assignment, some get half assignments, etc. It gets really complicated really quickly to keep track of all of these kids.

Normally, I would have anywhere from three to 10 of these students out of my total 180, but because I actually did keep up with this paperwork and parent contact in years past, I was given close to 40 of these students this year. I thought it would be the year that broke me for sure. To top it all off, I was given the queen bee of discipline issues for that sophomore class. Words escape me when trying to describe her, but a coalition of her teachers got together frequently to brainstorm new ways to try to control this student in the classroom because by ourselves we felt literally helpless. Watching this tiny little person yell and argue with teachers who towered many feet over her was as hilarious as it was disheartening. The only silver lining was that I saw her a couple years later and she did a 180-degree turn; she's now a mature and tolerable person who can laugh at how insane she made us feel.

Needless to say, by this year, I was so tired I could barely remember names, so I just gave the students nicknames based on how they made me feel. One kid's name was "happy," another was "annoyed," and yet another was "be quiet stop talking."

(Students picking team names for review game)

Me: What's yall's team name?

Team: We don't know.

Me: Fine, W.D.K.

Student: What's that stand for? Where Da Kids?

Me (confused): We Don't Know.

Student: So then it should be W.D.N.

Me: Oh…No…No…that's not good. It's only the start of the year.

* * *

(I finish introductions and class rules)

Me: Any Questions?

Student: I heard you were a hit man.

Me: No, I'm not an assassin.

Student: You kind of sound like you could be.

Me: Then you better stop asking questions.

* * *

Me: Put your phone up.

Student: Ok. *(Accidentally drops phone.)*

Student: Coach, did you see that?

Me: What?

Student: My phone bounced on the desk and was fine.

Me: That's lucky.

Student: No, watch! *(Drops phone. Screen shatters.)*

Me: Well…that was stupid.

* * *

Student: Coach, when am I going to use this in real life?

Me: This? Geometry? This, I don't know, but if you don't pass my class you'll never "get" to real life.

Student: Dang bro, you're right.

Me: Don't call me bro.

(We're all working on a worksheet after the lesson.)

Student: Coach, if you get arrested for drugs do you lose your scholarship to college?

Me: Probably.

Student: So I shouldn't smoke weed?

Me: Logically, not if you're trying to get a scholarship then right?

Student: Well, and then it means you instantly get addicted to crack, right?

Me: ...Sure?

Student: I don't want to do crack.

Me: This is not where I thought this conversation would go, but yes that is a good life goal. Don't do crack.

* * *

I love listening to music in my classroom. I feel like I am opening these kids' minds up to stuff they would never have heard or listened to on their own. On this particular day I was playing something by Pearl Jam.

Student: Coach, can you please play Drake?

Me: No, Drake is not the only musician y'all should know. You always want Drake!

Student: No, it's the guitars.

Me: Please explain.

Student: Guitars make me itch. They sound like screaming elephants.

Me: I'll play some Guns N' Roses, I don't think it has guitar.

Student: Thank you!

* * *

(Student raising hand for the 80th time asking me to repeat a direction that is written on the board)

Me: Are you going to ask me something about the directions I just said because you weren't paying attention?

Student: Yes.

Me: Put these on.

Student: What are these?

Me: Safety glasses, some kid in shop left them in here.

Student: Why am I putting them on?

Me: Because I can't promise I'm not going to throw things at you.

Other Student: He does love us, if he didn't, he wouldn't care about your safety.

* * *

Student: Coach, can you put in a good word for me when I try out for tennis next year?

Me: You want me to put in a good word with myself?

* * *

Me: What geographic obstacle separates France and the United Kingdom?

Student: The great wall!

Me: What? No.

Student: The great wall of CHINA.

Me: Still no.

Student: Great Wall of China.

Me: The word "The" was not the issue.

Other Student: The Berlin Wall.

Me: It's not a wall!

* * *

Student: Coach, I saw you over break.

Me: I know.

Student: How did you know?

Me: We were at the grocery store. You looked right at me and said, "Hey Coach," and I said hello and that I hope you had a good Thanksgiving.

Student: Oh, I didn't know if you saw me or not.

Me: We were 5 feet away from each other. We made eye contact!

* * *

I cannot clearly express in this short book the level at which smartphones are destroying teenagers. It is like having an addict try and sit through anything with an ounce of cocaine right there on the desk and asking them to focus on the lesson instead. They are instantly connected to all their friends, their friends' friends, every idiot viral sensation, and to top it all off, their parents are texting them throughout their classes constantly. It's insanity. The only fun part is when I take them up and see the nonsense that these people actually try to pass off as a conversation.

(From a phone that I picked up when one of my female students was supposed to be working)

Text From Boy: ...should've done eat we did yesterday.

Text From Boy: *Wat

Me to Girl: Is this your boyfriend?

Girl: Yes.

Me: He accidentally auto corrected and wrote "EAT" and then corrected it himself to the non-existent word "WAT."

I text back: You mean "*what."

Text From Boy: Wut?

Me to Girl: You need a new boyfriend.

* * *

As stated previously, not all students will use geometry, but it's about being logical, following steps, and problem solving when those steps don't seem incredibly clear. It is honestly quite frustrating dealing with people in the real world sometimes, because I know, had they been students of mine, I would have corrected anything I could have before they went on to adulthood to create havoc for everyone else.

I lost my credit union credit card in a move many years ago. They don't mail me bills unless I have a balance so I haven't worried about it, but for my own sanity, I wanted to cancel the card and get a new one because I wanted to start using it again and to know that the other wasn't in anyone's physical possession.

Me: I need to cancel my card, it's lost.

Them: Alright sir, what's the card number?

Me: I don't know. It's lost.

Them: We can't cancel a card if we don't know the card number.

Me: How does anyone report a card lost or stolen if they need the number that has been lost or stolen?

Them: I'm sorry sir, I don't know.

Me: How is this an issue that has never been raised before?!

Them: …I'm sorry sir, do you know the card number?

Me: All I have to do is steal a bunch of your credit union cards and go on a spending spree because no one will be able to report their card lost or stolen.

Them: Do you need to report your card stolen?

Me: Yes, lets try this.

Them: I need your name.

Me: Euclid Pythagoras.

Them: I'm having trouble finding you.

Me: Can we use my social? My address? My phone number?

Them: Do you know your card number?

Me: I do. I've just been trying to give you a hard time.

Them: Ok, what is it sir?

Me: I'm being sarcastic.

Them: Oh.

Me: This really makes complete sense to you all? You've never ever questioned this process?

Them: I don't understand.

Me: Never mind, y'all are insane.

* * *

Some teachers have inspirational quotes on their board for when students come in to read and be all positive. I did that for a while. It ended up just confusing kids. I'd lose almost 20 minutes at the beginning of every class trying to explain what the three or four syllable words meant. So I would typically have this on my board instead.

"What it is like to teach you all.

It's like starting a 90-day, 1000-mile marathon, where you also need to teach the spectators things, but they're all staring at their phones, and barely know where they are. Then the last 3 days of the marathon you are forced to sprint non-stop, and the spectators become zombies, and the zombies' parents become zombies too, and all the zombies are trying to eat you and negotiate their grades with you at the same time, but no one knows their grades and you're also on fire."

* * *

While poring through old posts, I found this one. Every teacher everywhere will understand this little blurb as clear as day.

Average number of students in tutorials throughout the school year: three

Number of students in tutorials at the end of the semester: 5 billion

* * *

Me: Stop rapping and finish your work, your rap is terrible.

Student: That's mean. One day coach I'm going to make a million dollars.

Me: Rapping?

Student: Yeah, and then I'm going to give you a million dollars.

Me: That's stupid.

Student: Why?

Me: Then you'd be back to zero dollars!

Other Student: That's why you need math.

* * *

(Lesson involving ratios)

Me: Does anyone know what the 3/5th's compromise was?

Students: *Silence*

Me: Seriously? Aren't you all learning this in History?

Student: Fine. It's when they dumped all the tea into the ocean.

Me: Never mind, I'll stick to teaching math.

* * *

Student: Coach, if we get 10,000 retweets, can we all exempt the final?

Me: No.

Student: But Coach, that's like a million people!

Me: It's like 10,000 people.

* * *

I think it is almost par for the course that teachers just generally complain about pay. Everyone who hasn't taught just generally assumes that for around $45,000 per year, you should be happy because you get an enormous amount of time off and a decent salary right out the start. But once you actually get into the nitty gritty of teaching, realizing that you are teaching for a full eight of those hours per day, planning for another two of them and grading for another three to 12 hours per week (if you are coaching add another two to six hours per day depending on whether it's game day or not)…it really isn't that much.

Yes, we don't do it for the money, we do it for the ability to change the world—to make a difference. But just think about how much more of a difference that we could make in this world if all of us teachers were driving Ferraris and eating healthy meals instead of dollar menu fare and cars with bald tires?

Online Post From December 2015:

Driving home from the grocery store, lamenting how much it costs to just eat. One of my 15-year-old students drives by in his brand new Lamborghini and waves at me.

* * *

You probably remember being in school and having to carry around fake babies to see how great a parent you would be. That hasn't changed. Schools still do that. We teachers have to sign off each period that the student did in fact bring in the child, and for better or worse, not abuse it.

Our school happens to fill the babies with seed or flour or sugar. I can't remember exactly, but I do remember there being fake babies bleeding their fake blood all over my classroom constantly. I don't know why these students were causing such lacerations on their children, but I would not trust a single one with a child based on my observations of them with these fake offspring.

Student: Can you sign this paper nominating me for parent of the year?

Me: Didn't you leave your fake baby in my class for 25 minutes the other day without even knowing you had lost your baby?

Student: I've only lost my baby once.

Me: I've never lost MY baby.

Student: Whatever, can you just sign?

Me: Where is your baby today?

Student: Oh crap, I left him in my locker!

* * *

Student: Coach, can you sign off that I took care of my baby?

Me: Where is it?

Student: In my backpack.

Me: So your baby is dead?

Student: It's just in a backpack...

Me: And babies don't suffocate?

Student: It's not a real baby, why are you being difficult, just sign the paper?

Me: Why are you being a terrible mother and keeping your baby in a backpack?

* * *

Student: Coach, I am going to take such good care of this baby.

Me: Awesome. Go sit down.

(25 minutes after class has ended)

Student bursts into my class: COACH I LOST MY BABY!

* * *

You can't fail a kid on purpose, even as much as you want to. There is just too much of a paper trail, and you're kind of an ass if that is what you have to do. It's easier to ruin their holidays, or get their phone taken away, or know that they owe you and cash in on those favors later when they are working somewhere you want the employee discount at. You can sometimes have a Nerf gun in class and shoot them with it to wake them up, but in today's highly litigious society, you can be sued for just about anything, including shooting a kid with a Nerf gun because now they have PTSD.

With that said, I still enjoy the occasional prank on my students so it all feels a little more tolerable. Lord knows they are constantly trying to push me to my limits for their enjoyment, so it's only fair I push back.

(Post from December 2015)

I told my class that to celebrate the last day of the six weeks I'd bring them all chocolate.

After passing out the chocolate and watching them place huge chunks in their mouths, they found out it was in fact 100% unsweetened dark chocolate.

Kids spitting outside the windows, in the trashcan, outside on the grass.

Small win.

* * *

Student: Coach, I need you to take my phone away from me during class, I don't pay attention.

Me: Why don't you just hand it to me at the beginning of class?

Student: I'll NEVER willingly give up my phone.

Me: Even if it means better grades?

Student: NEVER.

* * *

As a teacher, you observe a lot of different types of kids. These kids are raised in all sorts of different households. Sometimes the kids who are doing the best are raised in terrible environments. Sometimes it is the complete opposite where you can have the perfect home, but for some reason your kid is just a bad apple. Then there are instances like below, where the child has determined they will be the alpha in the relationship. Here is a hint: your child should never be the alpha!

(Picking up something at hobby store where a mom and teenage daughter are behind me in line)

Daughter: Mom, I want this.

Mom: You can get it with your own money.

Daughter: The hell I will! YOU WILL BUY THIS FOR ME!

Mom: Ok...

I left before I could see what in fact the daughter wanted so badly, but in my imagination I turned around and punched both of them in the head and did the world a favor.

* * *

Student: Coach, life would be easier without hands.

Me: Oh, please elaborate.

Student: I wouldn't always have to get my nails done.

Me: So go cut off your hands…

Student: That's insane!

Me: I guess you're out of luck then.

* * *

(Talking to friend at the gym)

Her: You teach middle school right?

Me: High School.

Her: Oh my god, but those things you write on Facebook about what your kids say.

Me: Yup.

Her: I feel much worse now.

* * *

(General Parenting Advice)

Parents, if your child is "sick" on nine out of 10 test days throughout the year, your child is a liar.

* * *

Student 1 to Student 2: My parents caught me smoking last night.

Student 2: That sucks, what happened?

Student 1: They got all mad, but then I got mad back.

Student 2: Are you grounded?

Student 1: No, they took me and got me a new phone.

* * *

Student: Coach, when are you going to get tatted up?

Me: I already am.

Student: Whoa! Really?

Me: Yup, I have all the names of the students I've buried out in West Texas on my back.

Student: Like just the names?

Me: It's a lot of names. Good luck on your quiz.

* * *

Student: Coach, do you hunt?

Me: People.

Student: You hunt meat for other people?

Me: I hunt people.

Student: For meat?

Me: Sure.

* * *

Student 2: Coach, do you want another kid?

Me: Yes.

Student 2: Are you going to try for a boy?

Me: A dragon.

Student 2: You're going to try for a dragon?!

Me: I think it'll happen.

Student 2: You can't have a dragon.

Me: Well duh, men can't give birth.

* * *

(During quiz)

Student: Is this circle circumcised?

Me: I highly doubt it.

Student: If the circle is circumcised then it is a right triangle right?

Me: If the circle is circumcised it has much bigger issues.

Student: It says right here that the circle is circumcised.

Me: How do we even know the circle is male?

Student: WHAT ARE YOU—ooooooh....circumscribed.

Me: There ya go.

* * *

Student: What can I do to get my grade up?

Me: Do good on the test retake.

Student: What if I get you a new gun?

Me: Do NOT get me a gun.

Student: Seriously, what kind do you want?

Me: No seriously, you are too young and someone will end up in jail.

Student: I'll just put it in the back of your truck so you won't bring it IN school.

Me: Still SUPER illegal.

Student: Ok, well just email my dad which kind you want and he'll get it for you.

Me: I'm not emailing your dad and asking him to get me a new gun.

Student: What about a scope?

Me: Why can't you get like a restaurant gift card or something?

Student 2: Wait, what about a Porsche?

Me: How are you all getting me these ridiculously expensive things?!

MY FIFTH YEAR - THE BREAKING POINT

Some statistic somewhere says that most new teachers last an average of three to five years before they burn out. I could feel it in year five. My bones told me that this was the year I might actually break and throw a kid through the cheap, barely glass windows I had in my classroom. The professional development week we had to attend before the start of the school year was a joke. They put all of us in a room and had us do worksheets that they thought the kids would enjoy. All it proved to me was that the kids would be miserable because I was miserable doing this.

For any of you professional development people out there in the world, we don't want to cut out pieces of paper for training. We don't want to do worksheets; we don't want to waste time. What every teacher wants to do is get their room ready so that they don't have to do it on the few precious weekends they have left before going to war teaching kids.

If you can't have them do that, the next best thing they'd like to do is play laser tag or paintball inside the school. Department vs. department. It's great team building and if you film it and show the students, they will think their teachers are awesome. You're welcome.

Year five felt like I was a senior teacher who knew everything already and who wasn't being challenged professionally. I even told my parents at open house that this was my fifth year teaching and I was probably going to be looking for a job after this year so if they wanted an awesome employee, I'd be available for hire. They laughed. I handed them my resumes on the back of their child's syllabus.

I must preface again that while I am super sarcastic with my students, I do try to develop a fantastic bond of trust and safety with them. It is imperative that they feel safe in making mistakes, otherwise they won't try. So while there are a handful of kids who may despise me, there are some that do everything they can to show how appreciative they are of me.

(One of my players walks by)

Me: You missed the tennis get together.

Her: It was my sister's birthday, we had cake, I'll get you some tomorrow.

(Next day)

Me: Where is my cake!?

Her: Oh my gosh, I totally forgot, I'll have my mom bring you some.

Me: Ha, I'm just playing.

Her: No for real. I'm going to have her bring you cake.

(After school at practice)

Her: Coach, come to my mom's car, she wants to talk to you.

Me: Ok.

Mom: When is your birthday?

Me: Not for months.

Mom: Well my daughter texted me and told me to bring you cake, I asked what kind, and she told me birthday cake, so I went out and got you a cake made thinking it was your birthday, until she told me that she meant a piece of my other daughter's birthday cake from this weekend. So I guess just have this entire cake?

Me: Awesome.

* * *

(To past student wandering the halls)

Me: What math are you taking this year? Remedial I bet.

Student 1: What's that mean?

Me: Umm...

Student 2 (laughing): He's calling you dumb.

Student 1: Coach, I'm super smart. I'm taking calculus.

Me: Except, you didn't know what remedial meant, so...

* * *

Student: Please can I go to the restroom? I have to pee!

Me: Finish those problems then you can go.

Student: It's an emergency, my uterus is about to explode.

Me: That's not how that works.

Student 2: You mean your bladder fool.

Student: Whatever, they're basically the same.

Me: You should really talk to someone about that.

* * *

Student: Coach every test should be open book, that's how life is.

Me: If you have to hire an architect to build your house, do you want the guy who has to keep looking in a book to figure out how to do it, or the guy who knows because he has studied and done it so much?

Student: But that doesn't apply to me.

Me: What you want to do?

Student: Pediatric oncologist.

Me: ...

* * *

Student 1: Archaeology. Is that even a real word?

Student 2: Yes.

Student 1: Like what is it? The study of arks?

Student 3: Like Noah's ark?

Student 2: Maybe.

* * *

(Student working on test review)

Student: Coach, how do I do this?

Me: Well what kind of angles are those?

Student: (rolls eyes / shrugs shoulders)

Me: Good thing that there is a multiple choice option for "shoulder shrug" on your test tomorrow.

Student: There is?

Student's Partner: No, you idiot.

Me: What she said.

* * *

(Beyonce's "Crazy In Love" playing in class while students work; one boy can't keep focused enough to do his worksheet)

Me: It's just a song, don't let it distract you.

Student: It's not just a song Coach, it's a lifestyle.

* * *

Student 1: I don't eat any meat.

Student 2: You're a vegetarian?

Student 1: Yes.

Student 2: So you don't eat chicken or pork?

Student 1: Just 'cause I'm black doesn't mean I automatically like fried chicken and ribs.

Student 2: So what do you eat?

Student 1: I eat vegetables a lot, and turkey necks.

Entire Class: What?!

Student 1: Turkey necks, like you eat around all the bone, it's awesome.

Me: You're not a vegetarian...

Student 1: I'm just like chewing the bone and stuff.

Me: So you're more like a canine instead of a vegetarian

Student 1: I guess yeah.

*** * * ***

Student: Coach, how do you spell carapa?

Me: What is that?

Student points to belt: It's a style of belt I am wearing.

Me before walking away: Oh. I think it is spelled C-R-A-P

Student starts writing that down: Wait...that spells CRAP!

Me: I've always been a bad speller.

* * *

Player: Coach, I can't workout. I hurt my knee.

Me: When?

Player: In the weight room Tuesday.

Me: How?

Player: When the treadmill flung me against the wall.

Me: How did you do that?!

Player: I didn't think it was on.

Me: You didn't think the thing moving super fast was on?

Player: Correct.

Me: How did you not think that was on!?

Player: I don't know.

Other Coach walking by: Do you drive?

Player: No.

Other Coach: That's a relief.

* * *

Student: What can I do to get an 80 for the six weeks?

Me: Nothing. You have a 73 and today is the last day of the six weeks.

Student (playing with stapler): What?! I can't do like a bunch of work?

Me: No.

Student: But coach, you know I'm smart! *(Leans on hand that is currently under stapler he is playing with. Staple goes all the way into finger)*

Me: Sure are...

* * *

Me to class: You all have a quiz today.

Student: Coach, I'll give you this Yeti cup for a 65%.

Me: You are a terrible negotiator.

Student: Fine 55%.

Me: Why are you attempting to bribe me for a failing grade on something that counts for less than 1% of your final average?

Student: So 65?

* * *

(Student does trick on my computer with his finger skateboard while I am trying to put in grades)

Me: I had one of those when I was your age.

Him: I bet you can't do tricks like me.

Me: I can do way better tricks than you still.

Him: Bet.

Me: Alright, give me your board.

Him: *(hands me board)*

Me: *(tosses little skateboard across the entire classroom into the wall)*

Him: *(mouth wide open)*

Me: I bet that was at least a 720! 900?

* * *

Student: Coach, what does wooden mean?

Me: Seriously?

Student: Don't you mean wood?

Me: *(stares blankly)*

Student: If I go into the hardware store and ask for a "wooden" they are going to look at me crazy!

Me: What does your paper say?

Student: Wooden, plastic, or fiberglass dowel.

Me: WOODEN MEANS MADE OUT OF WOOD!

* * *

Student: Coach, my quiz shouldn't count, the sub wouldn't help me.

Me: It was a quiz, she shouldn't help you.

Student: I just needed the definitions.

Me: Of what?

Student: Always and Sometimes.

Me: Huh? I don't follow.

Student: I don't get what they mean.

Me: Are you trying to make my head explode?!

* * *

(Online Post Feb. 2017)

It is physically impossible to teach a room of 26 teenage girls math on Valentine's Day.

* * *

Student: Are these the right answers?

Me: I can't help you, it's an assessment.

(Student walks away looking at others' papers.)

Me: Stop cheating and go sit down.

Student: I'm not cheating I'm just looking at their answers!

* * *

(Online Post Mar. 2017)

I have never had a student attempt to white out entire problems on a quiz so it would look like she missed less—feeling amused.

* * *

Me: How have you all not even done number one yet?

Student: I don't know.

Me: So, is it just laziness or general insubordination?

Student: Neither, we're just not cooperating with anything you want us to do.

Me: Your poor English teachers.

* * *

Me: I think my daughter is coming up here later.

Senior tennis player: O-M-G I love her. Is your wife coming too?

Me: Well, my toddler's little plastic car doesn't go fast enough, so my wife will probably have to drive her.

Senior tennis player: I'm going to miss your sass next year.

* * *

Student: Coach, did you get your wisdom teeth taken out?

Me: Yes, I had six.

Student: I don't need mine taken out.

Me: That's cool.

Student: But I want to. I wanna get on that gas and become famous.

Me: Great life plan.

* * *

Student: Coach, how much do you bench?

Me: I don't max out, my shoulder can't take it anymore.

Student: I do the bar and 10 lbs. on each side. How much is the bar?

Me: 45 lbs.

Student: So I bench 60 lbs.?

Me: You shouldn't be having trouble with those numbers...

* * *

Student: Coach, I can't see the board.

Me: Sit closer or make binoculars with your hands.

Student: That doesn't work

Me: Yes it does.

(Entire class makes binoculars with their hands)

* * *

Me: Do you have your progress report?

Player: No, I left it in my backpack.

Me: The one you're wearing?

Player: Umm…

Me: So do you want to show it to me or just start your laps now?

* * *

(Last week)

Student: Look at this picture, see all these snakes I caught?

Me: Why is your arm bleeding?

Student: They kept biting me until I let them go.

Me: You are not very good at that.

(Yesterday)

Student: I had a dream I got bit by a water moccasin.

Me: You should stop trying to catch snakes all the time. You're not very good at it. Even in your dreams.

(Today)

Other Student: Did you hear what happened to "Student"?

Me: No.

Other Student: He got bit by a water moccasin yesterday and had to go to the hospital.

Me: Well, he may not be a good snake catcher, but he can see the damn future.

* * *

Student: Do I leave this in terms of Pi?

Me: What do the instructions for that question say?

Student: Leave in terms of Pi. So do I?

Me: Are you really asking me if the directions for that question apply to that question?

Student: Yes.

* * *

Student: Coach, are you eating beef jerky?

Me: Yes.

Student: I love beef jerky.

Me: That's cool.

Student: One time, I ate a whole bag of beef jerky before I realized they were actually dog treats.

* * *

(I am walking down the hall toward my classroom and I spot two students at my door on the last day of school)

Student: Coach, I kept knocking on the door but you weren't there.

Me: Obviously!

* * *

Do you remember when kids would smoke cigarettes at school? They were the rebels. They not only were too young to be smoking, but they were just so blatantly supporting anarchy that they did it in school, attempting to mask the scent with lemons and absurd amounts of gum.

Kids don't smoke cigarettes in school anymore, or if they do, it is very few and far between. Some will still stick around the local corner store and see if they can score a pack, but most teenagers are of the mindset that cigarettes are bad for you. The cocaine and the LSD or random pills they get from the medicine cabinet are all OK, but cigarettes they aren't super keen on.

What they are keen on is vaping. They LOVE to vape. Electronic cigarettes are the new cool rebel thing to do in school. I know our admins are constantly taking these things away from kids. They modify them to take weed, and collect different flavors of e-liquid like kids used to collect baseball cards.

It's hard to hear the kids talk about it because what I want to tell them is that back in the day the real rebels smoked cigarettes in the bathroom, not some weird electronic toy, but I also don't want to promote smoking, so I keep my mouth shut except to make fun of how dorky they sound when they talk about how cool they're going to make their "vape" look.

Student 1: I'm going to get this supercharger on Thursday. I can't wait.

Student 2: That's going to be awesome, I can't wait to try.

Me: You work on cars?

Student 2: No for his vape.

Student 1: Shut up!

Me: Wait, you buy "mods" for your e-cigarettes?

Student 2: Yeah we have vape parties.

Me: Man, that does not sound cool.

Student 1: You wouldn't know.

Me: I mean, in my mind I can picture it, and it does in fact not look cool no matter what scenario I play in my head.

Student 3: You can do tricks and stuff, it is actually pretty sweet.

Me: Oh man, y'all are cracking me up, but you're all failing my class in the 40's so maybe do your work.

* * *

Student 1: Are there different versions of the test?

Me: Yes.

Student 1: Give me the same version as Student 2 so I can cheat off of him.

Me: Sure.

(Student's take test. Student 1 tries hard to make sure I don't see him cheating. I grade tests and hand them back the next day)

Student 1: I got a 30! How the hell did I get a 30?

Me: Because Student 2 got a 30. You copied off of Student 2, and he is an idiot.

Student 1: But I copied straight from him!

Me: What are you not getting? If Student 2 doesn't know the material, why would cheating off him make any difference in your grade?

Student 1: I don't know.

Me: Man, you're really bad at cheating.

* * *

(A different test is taking place a few months later. Same student.)

Student 1: Coach, are there different versions?

Me: Yes, just like the last 14 tests have been all year.

Student 1: Did you give me the same version as Student 2?

Me: I literally gave everyone around you the same version, except you. You have the only different version out of all of your friends.

(Students take test, I watch as Student 1 again tries to cheat.)

Me: Remember, the girl you are trying to cheat off of does not have the same test as you.

Student 1: I'm not cheating.

(Students finish tests, hand them in and get them back the next day.)

Student 1: How did I get a seven?!

Me: You cheated directly off of Student 2!

Student 1: But she is super smart!

Me: Yes, she is. You had exactly EVERY answer choice she had, but I told you, you had a different version!

Student 1: I thought you were messing with me!

Me: We've done this for literally every test man, can't you just attempt to try something on your own?

Student 1: No. I will beat you!

Me: You won't. Have fun in summer school.

* * *

Me: What's wrong?

Student: I got my vape taken up by the principals.

Me: How do your parents feel about that?

Student: My mom was mad. Now my dad uses it non-stop, says I did a good job modding it out.

Me: I've lost any useful advice at this point, do your work.

* * *

Student: Coach, do you like being a teacher?

Me: It definitely is exhausting, but it has its perks. What do you want to do?

Student: I want to do what my mom does.

Me: Which is?

Student: This guy pays my mom to be his girlfriend. Isn't that awesome?

Me: Umm…I don't know. It's the last day of school. I'm all out of wisdom.

* * *

I almost forgot to put the following event in this book. I don't know if it was just so absolutely farfetched that I shoved it deep down into my brain to hopefully never remember again, or because it didn't happen to me directly that I just honestly forgot about it, but I am glad I did remember because this needs to be in here.

It needs to be in here for two reasons. The first reason: it is just so absolutely ridiculous. You might have to read this next story twice just to convince yourself that you didn't misread it. I couldn't have made this up if I wanted to.

The second reason it needs to be in here is to show how addicted teens are to their phone and the insane lengths they will go to make sure they are never without it. They MUST have their phones. They all have burner phones. I have taken up sometimes three phones from the same kid in the same week. They just keep going back to the store to buy another one that their parent doesn't know about, or their friends give them their extras.

Now, I know we adults can be addicted to the technology in our pocket too. I've got my phone on me most times, but I'd be ok without it for a bit. I might even welcome the experience of detaching from the world. While I have hit on the subject of teenagers on their phones being an issue us teachers have to battle on a constant basis, this story shows just how far this phone addiction goes:

On a beautiful sunny day, a lovely student (we'll call her Student Bravo) gets her phone taken up. The phone goes to the AP office, her mother comes and gets the phone for a fine of $20, and the mother, as punishment, holds the phone from the child for the week. That same week, Student Bravo goes and buys a burner phone using money she got from who-knows-where, and ends up getting that taken up too. She knows if her parents find out that she has a secret second phone, she'll be in even more trouble. Now, this happens at some point earlier in the day, so the phone is sitting in the teacher's desk waiting to be sent to the AP office after school. Student Bravo knows this. Student Bravo throughout the day attempts to ask a thorough amount of my students, and any other students with classes near the one where her phone resides, if they will sneak into that teacher's room, into the teacher's desk, and get the confiscated phone after school. When students ask how they'll get into the room without the teacher knowing, Student Bravo says that she will create a distraction. A distraction such as releasing a mouse in the classroom? Pulling the fire alarm? Nope! This distraction happens to go one step further. This student waits until tutorials after school, and then proceeds to start a large fire inside a bathroom trashcan, activating fire alarms and a school-wide evacuation... an evacuation that was supposed to give the other student the chance to go steal the phone back. The problem is, they are caught almost immediately using the 900 cameras, and since it was after school and there weren't a ton of kids around, the two kids running in the hall was a dead giveaway. The fire was put out, no one was injured, the bathroom needed some remodeling...but the student did commit arson, all because of a stupid cell phone.

I have seen students pay upwards of $20 to borrow a friend's phone in order to log in to social media for five minutes because their parents took their phones away. Students will pay other students to make their phone a hotspot so they can tether their phones to their data because their parents shut their data off. These teenagers need to be on their phones otherwise it is like you are taking away their lives. Without an online presence they don't know how to live or communicate. I am sure you see it with your friends, sitting on their phones out to eat, kids with ear buds in their heads while their parents drive them to school, family outings where everyone is staring at a screen and all they can talk about is what is trending on their accounts.

Teens are not measured by their personal worth and character, but by the number of followers and likes, and sometimes they'll do whatever necessary to get those.

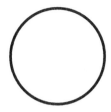

INSPIRATION

Most of these pages have been fun, sarcastic, and just a general cacophony of the nonsense that probably every single public school teacher has heard in even the shortest of tenures. I just had the tenacity to record a bunch of them.

Students, specifically young teenagers, have probably always said an enormity of dumb things. I don't think students have necessarily become dumber. I think they look up to different role models. I think they are bombarded daily with false information, just like a ton of adults on the internet. I think all they want to do is go viral. It has got to be hard being a teenager and not knowing if what you're reading is parody or real, or if the person writing the article even has a clue what they are talking about. They're kind of just swimming in a sea of virtual chaos.

I've told my classes that I don't envy them. They are almost forced to grow up faster than they should. They can't escape the bullying at school because it continues online. They can't not see the girl or boy's face they have a crush on; they're plastered all over social media. They can't get a break unless they live completely offline in the woods raised by animals.

I don't envy parents right now either. Their kids are so glued to electronics and cell phones have made access to sex even easier. If I wanted to talk to a girl when I was in high school, I had to call on the landline and hope that my parents or hers weren't on the other line listening. If I had naughty thoughts, I couldn't just text them to the person in poorly worded text speak, I had to wait and write it in a note and give it to them later hoping it didn't get taken up or passed around to the wrong people. I could at least escape it all for a bit and not worry whether some insane meme was being made of me in the middle of the night and if all the school would be talking about the next day.

While I do love to pick on my students, they understand that at the end of the day, I've got their backs. You've got to understand. The divorce rate is through the roof. Some of these kids, I can watch them be one person at a single point in time, and then over the course of a week becomes completely different. A deep sadness develops over them—a sadness much different than any typical teenage "emo" phase. Maybe they are happy that their parents finally split, but most of the time, they are keenly aware that their parents are miserable and they either feel responsible or blame someone. They rarely handle it well, so sometimes a teacher is their father or mother figure. Sometimes that teacher is all they have, whether we want that responsibility or not.

(Post from sometime in 2015)

I usually post about the ridiculous sarcastic things I do with my students, but in honor of Ann Wilson, one of the best teachers I ever had passing, I'll be inspirational instead. Today is the last day of the six weeks, of course I have the same kids as I always do begging and pleading in tutorials to bump their 30 to a 70, but one kid, they've been in tutorials every time the last two weeks just trying to get by. They studied their heart out for the last test and got a 40, failing for the 6 weeks. They then kept coming so that they may pass the retake. After 30 minutes today, they came up and handed in the re-test, completely blank.

Student: Coach, I can't do it.

Me: Yes, you can.

Student: I suck at math, just let me fail.

Me: Go finish it.

Student: Tutorials are over, I failed. My parents don't care.

Me: Stop feeling sorry for yourself. I've seen you do the work, I've watched you. Yes it may take you longer, but it's in that head of yours. Everyone has let you quit, everyone has told you you suck at math. Stop believing them and start proving them wrong.

Student: But—

Me: You will sit and finish this test and you will get everything right or we'll sit here until class starts tomorrow morning trying.

One and a half hours later, after plenty of tears, all of those 18 questions were right. That student's mom came up to me later that week. I had never met her before. She walked up to me and hugged me, started crying all over my shirt; students inside during tutorials had no idea what was happening. This mom's world had fallen apart. They were living in a car in a parking lot, written off by most of society, but a simple act had their faith in humanity restored. I tried to tutor the mom in math via email or in person so she could finish her associate's degree. Years later I ran into them again. They were living in a rental house in a good part of town. Did I help in that journey? Maybe. Maybe not. But would I have been happy with myself if I just let that kid quit and then find out later everything I knew?

As miserable as teaching can be, you need to realize, there is this crazy feeling you get when you know you actually changed a kid's life. When you know that your name, your class, will be one of the few memories they carry with them from high school. My students won't remember geometry, but they'll remember the nickname I gave them. They'll remember the time I stayed an extra couple hours after school so that they could get the help they needed. They'll remember the time that I showed up to one of their games many hours after I should have gone home. Many also won't. My name and class will be a forgotten memory. Of the thousands of kids who have passed through my class and team, I might make a difference in 10 or 12 of them a year, but it was more than I was doing bartending or working in energy.

Many adults see teachers as failures. We couldn't do anything else, so we taught. We settled on a safe and boring career, right? The students see that too. They see the photos of me as a little skater kid just like they are now, and they fear that they will end up just a teacher. But one of the beautiful things is that your legacy will keep going if you did it right. Someone somewhere will have been inspired just like I was, and maybe they'll go on to tell a story about me and inspire someone else, and a hundred years from now, if humanity hasn't destroyed itself, some 20-something-year-old teacher will throw a phone they took up across the room for the kid to catch and watch as sheer terror shines in that student's eyes when it hits the wall and falls to the floor only to realize their teacher took the case off and threw that instead. Classic.

I have a corner of my room covered in thank you notes, thank you cards, happy birthday cards, and long pages of letters from students who never spoke all year long telling you that you were the one thing they looked forward to every day in a very dark year. Letters thanking me for teaching them how buying a house works, or the correct way to write a resume, or the right way to ask out the girl or boy they have a crush on. I even have letters thanking me for being hard on a student or failing them. They realized as they got older that someone finally said, "You suck right now. Be better!" instead of just passing them along like a part on an assembly line. If you do get the chance to teach, take it, at least for a little while, and try and see if you can get that spark. It's something that stays with you forever. Those notes keep me from quitting most days, because most days you're taken for granted, but like I said, there are always a handful that actually NEED you.

I'm finishing this in the year 2017. It has spanned my experience over five years, and oddly enough, it seems like we are going backward in society. I feel more racial tension than ever before. The kids used to be somewhat immune. They were growing up in a time of tolerance and science, where being gay or straight, black or brown, Asian or redneck didn't matter. But I can feel a more sinister underlying in some kids. I can see they have parents who say snide remarks about other people, who push a stereotype, who say very hateful things, or live in a world they believe started only 2000 years ago. Do you know who is on the front lines trying everything they can to destroy those walls and false beliefs? It's your kids' teachers. There is a ton of hate out in this world, but the good ones are just trying to make your student into the best version of themselves, no matter what crappy software was installed in them previously.

Student: Coach, you're Jewish?

Me: Yes.

Student: Did you know I was Muslim?

Me: No, should it matter?

Student: I thought all Jews hate Muslims. Does that mean you hate me now?

Me: No, that's ridiculous.

Student: I was taught not to like Jews.

Me: Did you like me before you knew?

Student: Yes. You're the only teacher I like.

Me: So what does it matter what color or race or anything I am?

Student: I guess it doesn't.

Me: Exactly.

Student: My entire world just turned upside down.

FIX THE SYSTEM

It would be asinine of me to write an entire book poking fun at all the dumb things my students have said and complain about the education system without actually offering my thoughts on how to fix it.

First of all, do not let a single person make any sweeping decision regarding education who has not actually done some time in the classroom. You can study and get every degree you think is necessary to make you qualified to administer those decisions, but until you've sat in front of 30 teenagers and tried to push any amount of information down their throats, no one is going to believe you actually know what you are doing.

Secondly, it's not working. It isn't really working anywhere in public education, not as well as it could be anyway. Students are not prepared for college; they are barely prepared for the real world. They have almost no idea what it is like to think for themselves and problem solve real problems, like how to pay rent or how to advance an idea they have for some new invention.

I get that students need to learn how to learn, but they aren't going to learn how to learn in a math class they have failed four times because they hate math and all they want to do is video production. But the state says they must take this math class and pass this standardized test otherwise they must stay in high school a miserable failure to themselves and all their peers, absolutely demoralized.

Imagine a student who wanted to become a veterinarian, and by sixth grade was able to take at least two or three elective courses a year having to do with becoming a veterinarian. By the time that student went to college, they'd be halfway to their dream. Instead, now, they must sit through a ton of stuff they don't appreciate, and will only learn to loathe it all, and maybe give up on that dream along the way because everything else got in the way.

I can see the disagreement already: "Life isn't a straight shot to your dreams, life is hard and they should learn to survive through the bad stuff in order to earn the good stuff!" That's very "American Dream" of you, and I am a big proponent of learning to survive and roll with the punches, but we overload these kids with so much nonsense right now that their dreams are a muddled crayon picture at best by the time they graduate, instead of a fine-tuned portrait that has been nurtured for seven years before college.

I talked about how some of these kids go to school because it is an escape from home and nothing else. For some it is the only chance they are going to get to eat that day. Imagine if it were that for you—would you want it to be something you ONLY looked forward to because it was an escape? Wouldn't you want it to feel like the springboard to your future?

There is so much content packed into these classes that it becomes watered down. You're not really learning anything to its full potential. You're just skimming by, warming a seat for the next student to be spinning his toy or checking his phone to see if someone else posted a new selfie of how bored they also were in class.

Every teacher is competing against an overloaded (and often terribly worded) scope and sequence, but even worse, cell phones. Cell phones ruin everything. They make cheating extremely easy. They make sending and getting nude photos of your classmates incredibly easy. They give every student the option to reach out and play thousands of games when they should be learning. They could be a great research tool, but instead they are ruining the grammar and spelling of everyone everywhere.

If we want school to actually create better humans, we need to change it from the stale model it has been for the last hundred years. Pay teachers a great wage so that you have great people fighting for the jobs, then you can be picky and not hire the ones that you don't have a great feeling about. Don't hire the ones that you feel might end up on the news but need to hire because no one else wants the job. Teachers are usually family-oriented. Don't make their insurance premiums half of their paycheck so that the other family member must also work just to make the mortgage payment. Invest money in more schools, so classrooms aren't packed with more than 18 kids. Students want to know their teacher. They want to know the person who is trying to guide them along the path they call their life.

You can't get to know your teacher when there are 29 other students in class all vying for attention. You feel like just another name on the roll, and as a teacher it sucks. I want to get to know my students and what makes them tick and what their morals and values are, but when you give me 30 students, I'm just a glorified babysitter trying to get everyone to stop talking for three seconds so the couple of kids who want to get an A can hear the directions.

Do you know what happens to the bad influence when they are one of only 15 kids in a classroom? They are much less likely to act out, and the teacher is much more likely to connect to that student somewhere down the line and make them better. Do you know how happy a teacher is after they grade 180 tests? Not happy. They want to punch holes in walls IF they still have an ounce of energy left in their body. Imagine only having half that amount of tests. You'd maybe not have to take your tests home to grade, students would get their work back faster, identify mistakes faster, and you could give more quality feedback instead of just a sad face or half-assed smiley face next to their grade.

Lets pretend there are more schools, better teachers, and healthcare becomes something actually affordable. You create a healthier and more educated population. A population that would go on to solve more problems than it creates. A population not burdened by stupidity and ignorance, and one that doesn't have to worry if a trip to the ER will bankrupt them.

You can try and legislate problems away, but as long as people aren't corrected on the nonsense they think is real, you'll always have battles between two very confused sides. As long as people are miserable in their careers and were never given the chance to thrive in an area they thought was worthwhile, you'll just keep that negativity going.

I can't tell you all the logistics right now, but we need to have STEM schools, visual arts schools, and internships for high school kids at startups where they work with project managers so they can see the problems they'll need to take on and solve when they get a bit older. Take these students all over the world. America is not the end all of places. There is no better way to end ignorance like seeing other parts of the world, experiencing different cultures, and meeting people who were born into completely different circumstances than you and I ever thought possible.

Think about it this way: in fifth grade, I was able to take art classes at a university. Later in that same grade after art class was over, I was able to take basic computer programming and create an actual game. In sixth grade I was able to learn how to solder and build solar power cars; then later that same year I was able to learn how to edit video using a computer and a VCR and some very powerful computing equipment at the time. These classes were taught by professionals in the actual field who wanted to give back. There are so many of these professionals willing to give back and share what they have learned. You don't even need to hire them full time, maybe an hour a day for a six weeks if they even want to be paid. Imagine being taught landscape design in seventh grade by an actual landscape designer, learning things that others learn in college or through years of actual experience. I took a class in eighth grade on city design, and we used SimCity to simulate our designs and run through scenarios to see if we actually made decent choices.

I was lucky in that my school district growing up decided to take a chance on these hybrid classes for a fortunate set of us. I learned more in those four years than I did in all of high school and college combined. I remember those teachers more clearly, and I remember those classes like they were yesterday. I don't remember junior year English class. I don't remember sophomore year World History. I remember learning to salsa dance in seventh grade during first period and I remember entering video competitions in eighth grade using fishing line and fancy transitions for special effects.

Schools need to become a place of knowledge for everyone of all walks of life, where they can learn what they want to learn, and learn skills applicable to this new and quickly changing world. It is the only way humanity comes out of this alive. Lets try and create a product that students want and the future needs, instead of forcing them into something they usually perceive as villainous and unnecessary. Don't make this something private either. Then you only further divide society; instead lets make the public better people. I want my daughter to know what elephants are when she grows up because a group of students figured out how to stop poaching. I want my daughter to know that the earth isn't dying, that a group of students got together and figured out a better way to build houses and cars without mining the earth to extremes and flattening out the rainforest.

Everyday there are amazing examples of kids who are doing everything they can to change the world, but we don't idolize them. We idolize the idiots who accidentally shoot themselves in the foot on camera and get a million views.

The conversations needs to change. This country needs to focus on its education more than anything else if it wants to not destroy itself. You know what I care about more than which gender uses which bathroom? Everything. I care way more about if my daughter will have to fight for clean water. I care more about if we can figure out why everyone is getting cancer. I care more about a child being able to grow up in a happy and healthy home way more than I care about if those parents are of a certain gender. I care more that health decisions are left up to the patient and their doctor instead of a group of out of touch politicians saying what you can and can't do. I care more that the veteran coming home can get the actual healthcare they were promised instead of being tossed aside to deal with their PTSD themselves. It makes ZERO sense the dumb crap we argue about as a country when there is so much we need to focus on. I don't know how to overhaul the system; I only know the type of school I'd like to have gone to and the type of school my students want. But we need to change the dynamic soon.

If we continue on this path, good teachers will continue to leave, students will continue to become complacent with their place in life and suffer from all forms of anxiety, the poor and unfortunate of them will keep falling through the cracks, and our problems will only continue to get worse. When our children's children look back to the past and wonder how we got to watering our crops with sports drinks, we don't want the dumb little conversations in this book to become the smartest conversations they remember...

THE END

ABOUT THE AUTHOR

Dr. Euclid Pythagoras holds multiple degrees ranging from a basic Masters in Business Administration all the way to a Doctoral Degree in Human Psychology, even including a rare online masters degree in Sarcasm from University of Phoenix that they created just for him.

During summers, Dr. Pythagoras lives on a small island in the Mediterranean with a set of rare teacup Great Danes named Bela and Mia, developed custom by the Japanese. At his small compound also live three micro-pigs all named Diego, bought from the famous Argentinian micro-pig breeder Areebah Cunningham.

Dr. Pythagoras has always been and will always be a strong believer in education as the forefront and solution to a better humanity. He continues to work on applications and design to help further that dream, and to stop people from believing the world is flat.

Your endless compliments, monetary offers, and unsolicited advice can be received at dreuclidpythagoras@gmail.com

Made in the USA
Middletown, DE
09 January 2020

82890763R00066